I0815315

THE WORLD OF DREAMS

Illustrations by Tommaso Vidus Rosin
Text by Sara Beltrame

whitestar kids

THE WORLD OF DREAMS

1. Introduction: Magnificent Darkness!

A good way to become invisible and do anything you want, without too much effort?

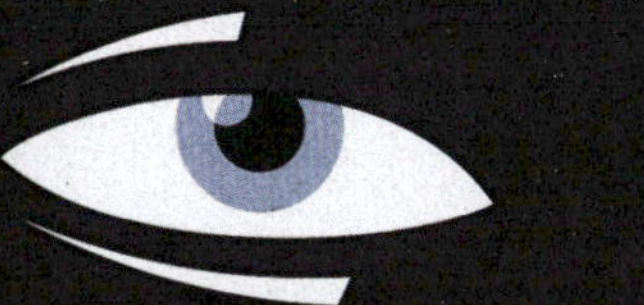

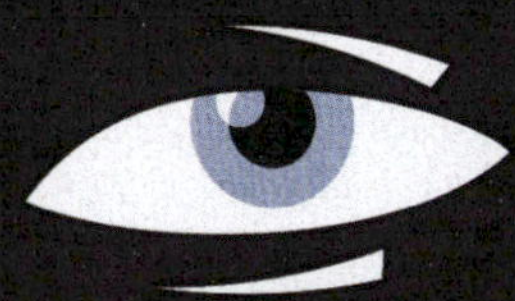

The darkness.

Do you have any idea how many things can happen in the dark?

For someone like me, I can guarantee that it would be a great gift to be able to be in the dark. I would like to invite you to spend a couple of weeks on my planet to get an idea.

An Earthling named Diana Kossakowski discovered it in 2023 and called it "B."

"B" is part of Cygnus, the swan constellation. It orbits the **Wolf 1069** star, and it is just 31.2 light-years from Earth.

B has one side that is always light and one side that is always dark. My family and I live on the **Light Side of B**.

When the mail carriers come to deliver our mail, they have to first check the directions to find out whether they have to go to Dusty Asteroids Street on the Light Side of B or on the Dark Side of B. So, basically, if you want to send me a letter, you must write "Dusty Asteroids Street, Light Side of B, Wolf 1069," etc. Otherwise, it will be sent to someone else. I don't know who, but believe me, it won't reach me.

I must confess that, with all this light pollution, it wasn't easy to find a corner of absolute darkness in which to land on Earth.

My parents had warned me: "Humans are afraid of the night and are obsessed by light. If they knew what it meant to always live immersed in light, they would turn off a light bulb every now and then!"

They were right, but in the end I succeeded. I was able to see stars in the darkness.

And now you're probably wondering what I'm doing here, looking for the pitch dark.

Well, it's about school.

I have to write a research paper entitled **"What I Miss"** and I chose the dark. I realized that a lot of things happen on Earth when the dark takes over from the light. One thing is truly extraordinary, considering that we Wolfians don't even have a word to define it, and it's something you sometimes even do with **your eyes open**.

You call it **"dreaming."**

I wonder when, exactly, the first human being realized they were dreaming. And what kind of dream did they have? And were they immersed in darkness, in a cave, for example? Maybe they were climbing a tree, leaning on a branch, balancing themselves to sleep. When they woke up, did they tell anyone about their dream? If so, who?

Maybe they dreamed of being an enormous mammoth who fell into a trap, of flying on the back of a pterodactyl, or of inventing a round thing that would change their life and that they would then call a **"wheel."**

We don't know.

2. The History of Dreaming

ALTHOUGH ARISTOTLE WROTE ONE OF THE FIRST BOOKS ON DREAMS IN 350 BC, THERE ARE NO TRACES OF DREAMS IN PRE-HISTORY, THOUGH SOME BELIEVE THAT THE DRAWINGS OF THE BISON IN THE LASCAUX CAVES ARE THE REPRESENTATION OF A DREAM.

Lascaux Caves

These caves are in France and were discovered in 1940 by four boys. They contain 6,000 figures dating back 17,500 years. The most famous are jumping cattle and a horse pierced by arrows.

Aristotle was deeply intrigued by how and why we dream. And can you blame him?

At that time, some believed that dreams were one of the ways for the Gods to communicate with people, but the philosopher did not agree with this theory because he knew that **all living beings dream**, even animals. And if this is true, why would the Gods—he asked himself at a certain point—also want to talk to animals?

It made no sense that dreaming was a way to communicate with the Gods. It had to have another use.

But what?

Oneiromancy

The "art of divination" is the ability to predict someone's destiny through the study of dreams.

Despite Aristotle's opinions on dreams, **the art of divination** based on the **interpretation of dreams** is widespread and found in every era and culture.

It's called **"oneiromancy."**

The **Sumerians**, in 3500 BC, designed **"incubators"**: underground and sacred places where people went to sleep to dream.

Things used to go more or less like this: a person who needed to make a **decision** went down to an incubator.

They would lie down on a kind of bed, in the dark, and close their eyes until they fell asleep, hoping to dream. When they woke up, they went back up the stairs and told their dream.

A priest deciphered the content of the dream and provided some ideas on the decision to be made.

In ancient times, there were some kinds of **dream dictionaries**, in which you could read about the meaning of your dream, depending on what it was. So, anyone interpreting the dreams did not have to waste much time in giving you an answer. They could just pick up the dictionary, check it, and give their own verdict.

In Mesopotamia, the **"Book of Dreams"** of the Assyrians is the oldest oneiromancy text found, while the **"Tablet of Susa"**—a handbook on the interpretation of dreams—dates back to the Middle Babylonian age.

Human beings are even capable, although living in places very distant from each other, of **dreaming the same things**. Obviously, the subjects of dreams have changed over time, and the common dreams of millennia ago are not the same ones people have now. Try asking your classmates what dreams they have, and you'll be surprised by the answers!

Not bad, eh, for an experience born in the dark!

3. Divine Dreams

BEFORE THE DISCOVERY—THANKS TO SCIENTIFIC PROGRESS—OF HOW AND WHY WE DREAM, EVERY CULTURE HAD ITS OWN IDEA OF DREAMING, BUT ALMOST ALL AGREED ON THE FACT THAT ENTERING THE WORLD OF DREAMS WAS LIKE CROSSING A THRESHOLD. AND WHERE THERE IS A THRESHOLD, THERE IS A GUARDIAN TO GUARD IT...

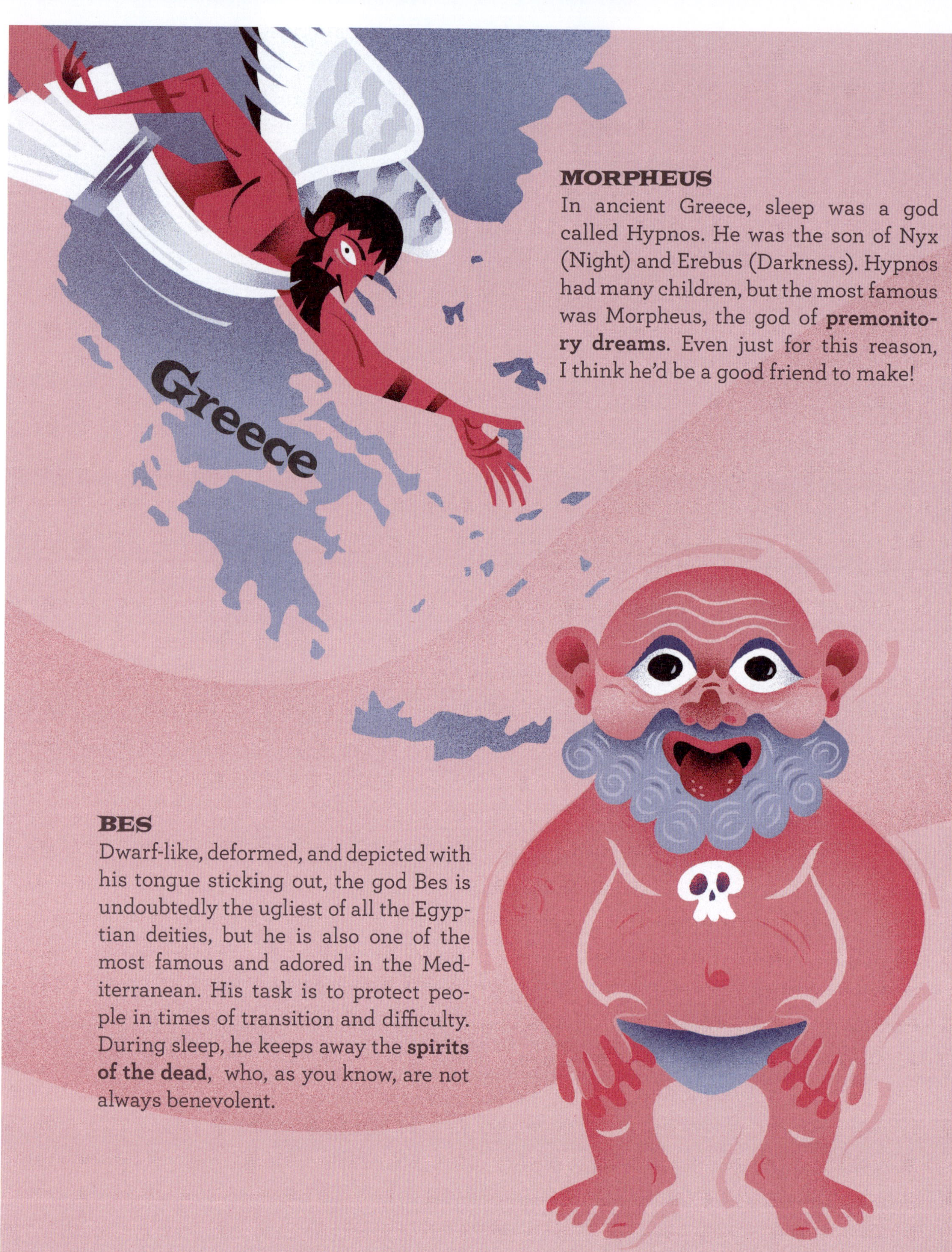

MORPHEUS

In ancient Greece, sleep was a god called Hypnos. He was the son of Nyx (Night) and Erebus (Darkness). Hypnos had many children, but the most famous was Morpheus, the god of **premonitory dreams**. Even just for this reason, I think he'd be a good friend to make!

BES

Dwarf-like, deformed, and depicted with his tongue sticking out, the god Bes is undoubtedly the ugliest of all the Egyptian deities, but he is also one of the most famous and adored in the Mediterranean. His task is to protect people in times of transition and difficulty. During sleep, he keeps away the **spirits of the dead**, who, as you know, are not always benevolent.

BAKU

In Japanese culture, Baku is a supernatural being greedy for dreams. He has the body of a lion, the head of an elephant, and the paws of a tiger. Despite his appearance, he's the one to call upon when you have **nightmares**; he'll immediately devour them, thus preventing them from coming true.

JASY JATERE

Jasy Jatere—the protector of the siesta (the afternoon nap)—is famous in Paraguay. His name means **"little piece of moon,"** according to Guarani mythology. Like the god Bes, he is short, but for many he is beautiful, being blond, curly-haired, and with blue eyes. He always carries some kind of magic wand with him. If anyone ever takes it away from him, he bursts into desperate tears!

OBATALA

Both male and female, old and young, Obatala is the father or mother of the **Orishas**—the gods of Yoruba mythology in West Africa—and of humanity. Obatala wears a white, luminous robe and is the god of thought and the guardian of doors and dreams. Seeing Obatala dance is hypnotizing, even in a dream!

It would be very interesting to meet at least one of these guardian gods, but to do so we still have to understand how to dream...

4. The Ingredients of a Dream

IN JAPAN, FALLING ASLEEP IN FRONT OF OTHERS IN PUBLIC IS NOT A SIGN OF RUDENESS. QUITE THE CONTRARY! THE PRACTICE OF "**MICRONAPPING**" IS SO WIDESPREAD THAT IT EVEN HAS A NAME: "**INEMURI**."

BUT HOW CAN THE JAPANESE DREAM IN SUCH A SHORT TIME?

IT APPEARS THAT **EVEN DREAMING NEEDS SOME ESSENTIAL INGREDIENTS**.

1 A quantity of darkness the size of a hug.
2 A bucket full of silence.
5 A handful of warmth in winter or four blasts of fresh air in the summer.

These are the essential ingredients, but the following are also handy:

- One or more cats purring near you.
- Any natural sound: flowing water, the sound of crickets, fire crackling, etc.

It's actually called "chirping," the sound of a cricket!

3 A hint of tiredness.

4 A nice comfortable bed.

METHOD

Close your eyes, start breathing regularly, and start sleeping.

Every human being on Earth spends a third of their life sleeping, and dreaming is a very important component of the **sleep cycle**. Making a quick calculation, we can conclude that human beings spend at least six years of their lives dreaming.

When the light comes, the magic ends, but when the sun goes down and the darkness takes over, your mind leads you again toward new, intense adventures.

Even if there's no apparent function to dreaming, it's how you put in order all the experiences you have had during the day.

Do you start dreaming as soon as you fall asleep?

No.

You only dream during the phase of sleep called **R.E.M.**, which means **"rapid eye movement."** During this phase, the eyes move very rapidly under the eyelids while the brain processes a large amount of information stored during the day. If someone wakes you up at this stage, you'll find yourself confused, dizzy, and not sure exactly where you are.

To reach the R.E.M. phase, you must first of all fall asleep (**phase 1**), that is, move from the waking state to that of sleep. The heartbeat, blood pressure in the veins, breathing, and eye movement slow down. Muscles relax and brain activity decreases.

Then you move on to **phase 2**, light sleep. This phase prepares you for deep sleep. All the body's activities, such as the brain, muscles, and heart, continue to slow down and the temperature drops.

It is in **phase 3** that you reach deep sleep, but only in **phase 4** do you reach effective deep sleep, in which your heart rate and breathing drop to a minimum. The muscles are totally relaxed, and the brain reaches its minimum peak of activity.

At this point, the **R.E.M. phase** takes over.

It's a strange moment because your brain resumes activity from a moment of almost absolute stillness, reaching levels similar to those of **being awake**. In this phase, the most vivid dreams occur. You dream of running, jumping, flying, playing musical instruments, swimming, etc., even if in reality your muscles enter a kind of paralysis and you remain still.

This happens so as not to run the risk of hurting yourself very much while dreaming.

But how many R.E.M. phases are there in seven hours of sleep? That is: how many dreams can you have in one night?

THE SLEEP CYCLE

The SLEEP CYCLE varies between 90 and 110 minutes and repeats four to five times in a night.

The R.E.M. phase appears between 70 and 90 minutes and lasts about 15 minutes. So, even if you have the sensation of having long and very complicated dreams, in reality you do them in those 15 minutes that you have available during the R.E.M. phase.

In one night, therefore, you could have between six and seven dreams.

When you wake up in the morning, you may either remember perfectly what you dreamed or even have the sensation of not having dreamed at all.

The most fascinating thing about the world of dreams is the different quantity of dreams that you are able to generate.

2
1
3
Off to bed!
5
Wake up!
4

5. Types of Dreams

ALTHOUGH YOU CAN HAVE INFINITE TYPES OF DREAMS DURING YOUR LIFE AND SIX OR SEVEN DURING A SINGLE NIGHT, DREAMS HAVE COMMON CHARACTERISTICS AND CAN BE GROUPED INTO **CATEGORIES**. THESE ARE THE MOST INTERESTING FROM MY POINT OF VIEW, BUT YOU CAN DEFINITELY DISCOVER OTHERS.

NIGHT TERRORS

This type of experience I wouldn't wish on my worst enemy! When you awake after having a night terror, you'll feel your heart pounding and be sweaty and terrified. There is no guarantee you'll remember what you dreamed, but you are quite likely to have the same dream the following night. Maybe it serves to get rid of some fear?

It's very likely!

FALSE AWAKENINGS

These are like some kind of labyrinth or matryoshka doll. You think you've woken up but you're still dreaming. Has this ever happened to you? Usually, you dream of thinking that you are awake to go to the bathroom, or you dream of making your bed, getting dressed, eating, etc., while in reality you are in full R.E.M. phase.

LUCID DREAMS

These are strange dreams because people know they are dreaming. Apparently, this skill can be learned. This is good news because if you are having a nightmare and are able to go from nightmare to lucid dream, you will know that you're only dreaming.

PREMONITORY DREAMS

They are definitely magical! These dreams tell you about something that is about to happen, sometimes in much more detail than "normal" dreams. This type of dream is probably the most studied throughout the planet and in all cultures. Who wouldn't want, for example, to dream about lottery numbers, play them, and win? Well, it looks like it happened to someone!

NIGHTMARES

Unless you have had a really unpleasant experience during the day or are very worried about something, you are unlikely to have nightmares. Nightmares are more annoying and scarier than bad dreams and are the manifestation of a dangerous or disturbing situation you experienced during the day. Having nightmares is a way to "download" your memory and feel a little lighter again. So, come to think of it... thank goodness they exist!

VIVID DREAMS

These are the dreams you remember as soon as you open your eyes. If you were to wake up in the middle of the night, after the first R.E.M. phase, it is very likely that you'll remember a vivid dream almost exactly as you dreamt it.

Sleepwalking

Even if you technically don't dream during sleepwalking, a sleepwalker performs actions such as walking, washing, and dressing while sleeping. At least 20% of people have experienced an episode of sleepwalking once in their life.

6. Famous Dreams

LET'S THINK OF THE DIFFERENT TYPES OF DREAMS AS ISLANDS THAT YOU LAND ON WHEN YOU FALL ASLEEP AND ENTER THE R.E.M. PHASE.

YOU TAKE A TRIP WITHOUT HAVING A MAP OR A CREW, AND EVERYTHING CAN REALLY GO WELL: YOU CAN HAVE BEAUTIFUL VIVID DREAMS AND WAKE UP CHARGED WITH ENERGY.

But you could also land on the wrong island and start having a terrible nightmare and then move on to a false awakening.

However, dreaming is always a positive experience if you know what to do with it when you wake up.

There are some dreams—and some nightmares—that have gone down in history because they literally changed it.

GOOGLE

Larry Page, the co-founder of Google, confessed that the idea for the search engine came to him thanks to a vivid dream. When he woke up, he told his best friend, Sergey Brin, about it, and voilà, it became one of the most used research tools of the digital age!

FRANKENSTEIN

You know that half-Hulk, half-zombie guy with screws on his temples? Yes! That's right, Doctor **Frankenstein**'s monster!

One day, **Mary Wollstonecraft Shelley** was invited by the poet Lord Byron to a challenge, together with other writers: they had to make up ghost stories. During the night, Mary had a nightmare about a mad scientist named Frankenstein creating a monster. As soon as she woke up, she didn't think twice before starting to write one of the best science fiction horror novels in the history of literature: "Frankenstein."

THE GODDESS OF NUMBERS
Srinivasa Ramanujan was a mathematical genius. He wrote formulas and functions until the day he died. The surprising thing is that he didn't go to school to learn the secrets of numbers, but actually studied them all by himself. To those who asked him how he managed to learn so many formulas and invent others, he replied that the Hindu goddess **Namagiri** dictated them to him in a dream. Surprising!

GOOD AND EVIL

Nightmares seem to be excellent resources for writers, so if you have one, as soon as you wake up, take a pen and paper and... start writing!

This is what Robert Louis Stevenson did in 1886 when he woke up from the most terrible of nightmares and began to write down the first sentences of **"The Strange Case of Dr. Jekyll and Mr. Hyde."** The book is as short as it is famous because it talks about the coexistence of good and evil in each of us.

YESTERDAY, TODAY, AND TOMORROW

"One morning in May 1965 I woke up with a lovely piece of music in my head. I thought: how wonderful!"

These are the words of **Paul McCartney**, who, at that moment, added some words to the melody, improvised words about scrambled egg. He didn't realize he had dreamed it until he asked his friends if they had ever heard that funny tune and they all said no. Thus was born the hit **"Yesterday,"** in the Guinness Book of Records for being the most recorded and reinterpreted song in the history of pop music.

NEEDLES AND CANNIBALS

What do a needle and a cannibal have in common?

They were the protagonists of a terrible nightmare experienced by **Elias Howe** in 1845. The man, who for days had been trying to solve some technical problems of his greatest invention—the sewing machine—dreamed of being captured by a group of cannibals who offered him an ultimatum: design the perfect sewing machine or die. When he was not able to perfect his invention in his dream, the cannibals begin to pierce him with their spears.

Howe, instead of reacting and opening his eyes amid desperate screams, fixed his attention on the tips of the spears and noticed that they were pierced. Waking up, he knew what he had to do to perfect his invention: pierce the needles of the sewing machine at the tip. In a short time, thanks to his nightmare, he became a billionaire.

7. Animal Dreams

ATTENTION!

HUMAN BEINGS ARE NOT THE ONLY ONES WHO DREAM. THE PHILOSOPHER ARISTOTLE NOTICED THAT HORSES, CATTLE, AND DOGS, AS WELL AS SHEEP AND GOATS, ARE ALSO GREAT DREAMERS.

ALL ANIMALS DREAM, AND WHEN I SAY ALL, I EVEN MEAN FISH AND SPIDERS (IT WOULD BE INTERESTING TO KNOW IF SPIDERS DREAM OF BEING SPIDER-MAN).

It's not easy to understand what animals dream about since we can't ask them when they wake up, but the fact that dogs whine while sleeping or move their paws quickly as if they were running is a clear sign that they dream, too.

This happens because they feel emotions, remember, use their imagination, and therefore process, just like you, things that happened during the day.

Chimpanzees sleep between five and nine hours a day. To be more comfortable and safer, they build a kind of bed of branches and leaves in trees.

Ostriches sleep just like this: standing up and with their eyes open to be alert in case a predator approaches. They usually sleep six hours a day.

Brown bats are the sleepiest mammals in the world. On average, they sleep 82.9% of the day, equivalent to 19.9 hours.

The most surprising animals from this point of view are **Sunda zebra finches**. These birds are known above all for their singing abilities, which they gradually refine right from birth. These birds practice and learn their songs **by repeating in their sleep** what they hear during the day. We can say that they experience real singing dreams.

Dolphins sleep with only half their brains to stay alert.

Elephants only sleep two or three hours a day. Apparently the bigger the animal, the less it sleeps.

The other curious thing that goes through my head when studying sleep and dreams in animals is the question of **hibernation**.

Many of them, both mammals and reptiles, have developed a technique to avoid starving during the winter months: they go to sleep.

LET'S HIBERNATE!

Temperatures are dropping and food is scarce, so Nature, very wisely, has proposed hibernation as a solution to otherwise unresolvable problems.

The vital functions of these animals are reduced to a minimum in order to remain alive, warm, in their burrows. Their heart rate also slows down to a few beats per minute, their body temperature decreases, and energy consumption is also reduced.

Well, one thing is certain: before going into hibernation, it's important to prepare.

For example, marmots begin to prepare by eating more than usual and filling their den with dry grass as early as September.

Hibernation lasts until spring. This means that they sleep for a whole three months but... how long do they dream?

Could it even be possible to have a dream for 129,600 minutes?

An answer has not yet been found.

What is certain is that all these discoveries regarding dreaming in animals have led us to think that the R.E.M. phase may have developed at least 450 million years ago.

8. Common Dreams

ALTHOUGH THERE IS NO WAY OF KNOWING WHO DREAMT THE FIRST DREAM OR WHAT IT WAS ABOUT 450 MILLION YEARS AGO, THERE'S ONE OTHER VERY CURIOUS FACT ABOUT DREAMS: HUMAN BEINGS HAVE **DREAMS IN COMMON**.

THE PODIUM

The most common subjects of dreams are **snakes**.

Given the lack of extremely venomous snakes in the Northern Hemisphere of planet Earth, the subject of the second most common dream comes from there: **teeth falling out**.

In third place comes **pregnancy**, in fourth place is marriage, and in fifth place is past loves.

In Haiti, the most recurring dream is cars, in Cyprus the sea. In Jordan, people dream of cutting their hair, while in South Korea, they dream of falling into water.

The most common dream in Chile? It seems to be mice!

Then there are really curious common dreams, such as dreaming of hats in Greece, stairs in Benin, squirrels in Namibia, peacocks in Fiji, and... **rainbows** in Bhutan.

9. Let's Sleep!

WITH ALL THESE INVESTIGATIONS DONE, THERE'S NOW ONLY ONE THING TO DO TO MAKE THIS RESEARCH TRULY SPECIAL: LEARN TO DREAM.

You can also dream simply by imagining wonderful things that you would like for others and for yourself.

This way of dreaming is also called **"desiring"** and **"having desires,"** and it doesn't seem complicated to learn how to do it if you have a bit of imagination and a lot of faith.

The very complicated thing is dreaming after falling asleep.

Even if you manage to fall asleep and dream, it doesn't mean that you will be able to **remember the dream**.

There are lots of different **techniques** and suggestions to fall asleep quickly, but will they work?

COUNTING SHEEP

This technique works unless... you feel like laughing. Often, as soon as you close your eyes and tell your brain to count the sheep, what happens is that most of them can't even jump the fence. The first gets into position for the jump but at the last moment runs free across the pastures, the other jumps but hits its head against the wood and loses consciousness, the third takes a nice run-up, is almost about to make it, but right at the moment of the jump, it sprouts a pair of white, furry wings and starts doing phantasmagorical twirls in the air.

How can this work?!?

COLD WATER

Washing your face with ice water before going to sleep helps to lower your heart rate and blood pressure, and consequently relax. Will you try?

FOUR SEVEN EIGHT

Breathing is one of the most effective techniques if none of the others works. There is a specific way of breathing to fall asleep and it is called "4-7-8." Position your tongue behind the incisors, inhale for 4 seconds, hold your breath for 7 seconds, and exhale for 8 seconds. By repeating the sequence three times, you should fall asleep in 57 seconds.

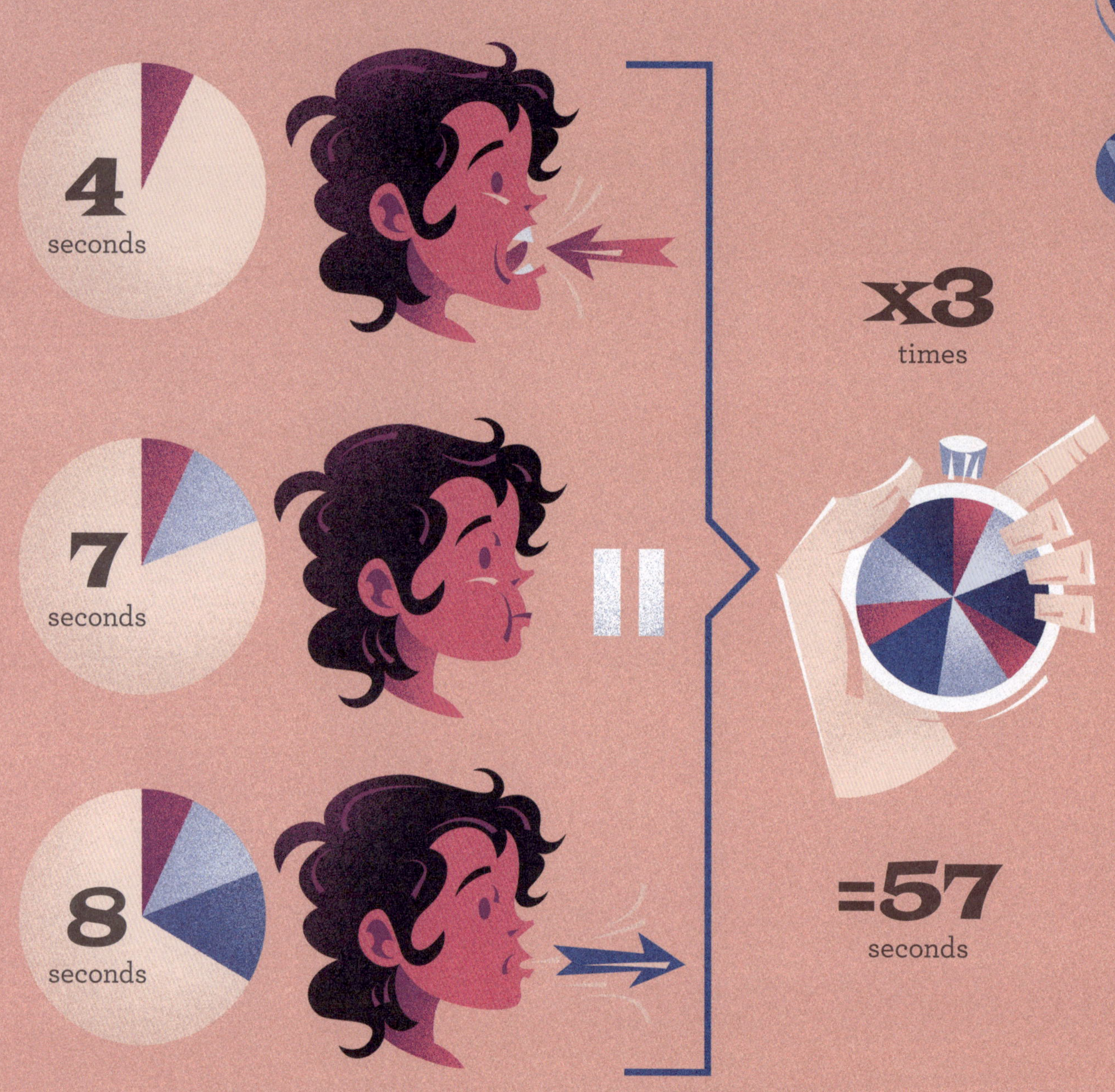

AWAY WITH THE SCREENS

If you don't fall asleep within 15 minutes, it is a good idea to get out of bed and do something, but stay away from digital screens. Associating the bed with a computer screen, a tablet, or a television is not a good idea for the body. The bed is not the right place to do these things and should mostly be used for sleeping or reading before falling asleep.

REWIND

If this doesn't work either, one foolproof way is to turn off the light, close your eyes, settle into the most comfortable position you know, and start thinking about the first thing you remember doing during the day.

Just like in a movie, mentally retrace, in great detail, all the actions performed, the people you met, the dialogues, the sounds, the thoughts, everything that happened to you.

There are people who don't even get to the second action of the day and have already fallen asleep.

This was the last method, and it sounds interesting! Let's try it together!

Let's lie down, close our eyes, and remember our day. So, I was on planet B this morning, I woke up, and...

...after stepping out of bed and not finding my slippers, I went to the bathroom and then down to the kitchen, where Mom and Dad had prepared a hearty breakfast for me.

They also started giving me endless advice about the journey that awaited me toward planet Earth.

A light breeze came in through the kitchen window, and I noticed that the sky was completely cloudless and was a beautiful **fuchsia color**, something that hadn't happened for at least a couple of weeks, given the interstellar disturbances of the previous days.

I gave Mom and Dad a kiss, then I put on my space suit and helmet, fastening it properly. I hopped into my shiny spaceship and while Mom was sayin-z**ZZZ** ...

But...
was it all
a dream?

AUTHOR

Sara Beltrame author, is originally from Treviso but has been living in Barcelona for some time. Her strangest dream is that of wandering the stairs of her apartment block in pyjamas, slippers and while holding a pillow under her arm and with a feeling of indescribable tiredness. Unable to find her own home, she falls asleep curled up outside the door of one of her neighbors. How embarrassing!

ILLUSTRATOR

Tommaso Vidus Rosin illustrator, is from Portogruaro but lives in Udine. At the age of thirty he had the most incredible dream of his life: he was Zorro. He had the moustache, the cloak, he could jump that high, ride his horse that fast, he was an expert swordsman, and bravely fought off the baddies. Then, he woke up.

WS whitestar kids™ is a trademark of White Star s.r.l.

Piazzale Luigi Cadorna, 6 - 20123 Milan, Italy
www.whitestar.it

Translation: Qontent
Editing: Abby Young

First printing April 2025

ISBN 978-88-544-2089-2
1 2 3 4 5 6   29 28 27 26 25

Printed and manufactured by Allied Fortune Times Limited (AF printing)
Dongguan City, Guangdong Province, P.R. China